Life's Purpose

Dr. Marius H Smit

BALBOA.PRESS

A DIVISION OF HAY HOUSE

Balboa Press books may be ordered through booksellers or by contacting:

Balboa Press
A Division of Hay House
1663 Liberty Drive
Bloomington, IN 47403
www.balboapress.com
1 (877) 407-4847

Print information available on the last page.

ISBN: 978-1-9822-4368-5 (sc)
ISBN: 978-1-9822-4358-6 (e)

Balboa Press rev. date: 02/19/2020

Dedication

I dedicate this book to my wife Marie who became the driving force behind me to start writing, encouraging me to not follow my dreams but lead it.

Foreword

It is my joyous privilege to wholeheartedly recommend this life changing booklet - Life's Purpose - of Dr Marius Smit.

I can assure each and everyone who reads this booklet, that the dynamic truths contained within its pages will explode in your hearts, bringing life changing results, as new hope, courage and guidance, flow from the pages of this booklet.

This booklet will help you to change the shape of your "world".

His life has not been limited to the usual or the ordinary.
He has experience both the pain, sorrows and hardships of life, and the joy of accomplishment.

He has a vision for what could be and a focus on results.
This booklet is therefore lessons in learning from a man who lives what he believes.

Dr Jacob. J. Roux PhD.
Founder and senior Pastor of Ashpah ministries. Strand, South Africa.

PART ONE

The Essence of Life

"Knowledge of happiness will unlock true freedom from within"

Happiness is probably the one word many a people around the world are desperately trying to understand. What is happiness? Where and how does it start? Is it something you can buy at your nearest street vendor? Do I find happiness in the clothes I am wearing, or the way I look, or has it something to do with my success in the business world?

Or is it the time spends with friends, having a good time, or maybe it is about your self-image, something we build, and unfortunately falsely learn to trust, that you think brings happiness to yourself and others since you think you are in control.

Or is it to run to your favorite liquor store buying your favorite drink, so that you can relax from the day's stressful work. But this is and actually must be a warning to let your mind fool you in thinking that having a drink, which is nothing wrong with, have the ability to relax you with the danger be that this drink can become a habit which then in the end leads to you be an alcoholic, and the sad thing is when you have reach this point, you will find ways of not let anyone find out about your problem, since it is embarrassing.

And here is the big problem. The essence of your life now will be about survival mode, which means your life just became a one pager, no story to share.

Which means all that your friends and co-workers can see and experience is the tip of the iceberg? Just like when an alligator surfaces before attacking his prey, all that is visible in the water is just the tip of the iceberg. But with the alligator the rest will come into play when he goes into full attack mode.

But with you it does not happen.

If your life is just the tip of the iceberg it means you are alive on the outside but dead on the inside. This means you do everything in your power to please your outward appearance so that what other people see and experience "your mirror image" is the opposite of what is going on inside of you.

And the problem with this is that after a while your mind tells you that this way of living is the norm, everyone else does it.

But you cannot use your outward appearance to hide what is going on in your inside, since this will eventually put you on a circle to nowhere, with your destiny, ultimate disaster.

This disaster can have many forms such as anxiety attacks, panic attacks, stress related sicknesses, heart failure, depression or the worst, "suicide" all because there is such a big void on the inside.

This is not the essence of life. We must become dead on the outside while being alive on the inside, which means whatever the "jungle" throws at you, it has no affect since you are at peace on the inside, all because you have found happiness on the inside which is the most precious jewel.

This level of happiness is all locked up in your emotional well-being

Our lives is suppose to be a collage, filled with different colors to express who and what we are and have become and the wonderful affect we had on people around us which means your life, your collage, will have a story to tell.

While watching a nature program I saw something that triggered a "pathway of hope" that I think can truly help with this topic of "happiness" which is the main ingredient to understand "the essence of life" and this is "Jungle Messages"

In this program they showed hunters of the tribe of Borneo who while walking in the jungle looking for food, they have a custom of sharing messages with other possible hunters coming the same way.

And since they don't have technology to use such as sending a quick message they use the jungle as their platform for this. And they do it by placing leaves in a bamboo that they have cut in half or small twigs also in this bamboo with each one telling a different message. One will be to say that a deer has been killed and whoever reads this has been invited to join.

Or another message will tell someone is in need of help. So whatever is going on in this jungle, whether good or bad, they will know because of these messages.

So the question is what is stopping you from sending a message out in your jungle for others to see. Don't get me wrong. I don't mean to advertise your problem on the inside on the nearest billboard. No it means to take time and get involved with people that can help you to not only cope with the challenges of your jungle, but to truly understand the purpose of life.

These hunters have perfected their way of not just living the jungle but that the jungle lives for them as well through these messages.

So yes the question for me and you is," Do you communicate with one other through messages, while being caught up in your jungle trying to find your way?

Is there someone or somebody out there with an open door waiting to answer your call?

Or do you have an "outlet" where you can get rid of the excess negative energy that has the ability to create toxins on the inside.

If we are to truly understand the essence of life that is within reach of everyone who so desires, then we have to do the "one week and not one day cruise" which means change from within will take time and lot of foot work, with the rewards something you only dream about?

If we are prepared to put in the miles for our careers, businesses, success in life then what is stopping us to take the time and listen to your message on the inside that so desperately wants to be heard on the outside.

Messages in the school of life play a major role in understanding the pathway to the essence of life, so therefore we cannot ignore the desperate outcry for help from the inside.

Take time to listen to your heartbeat, be aware of the dangers of self destruction, that ticking time bomb on the inside.

What we must understand and this is very important, is that "your heart is your book of life", and heart here talks about your emotional well-being.

The essence of life is not locked up in earthly possessions, the way you dress, your bank balance, your success etc. but rather in your emotional well-being.

Emotional happiness is the gateway to see, understand and appreciate the purpose of life waiting for you.

This is the most precious jewel anyone can become, but to reach this point you have to start somewhere with and end in mind.

So therefore take time to appreciate what is around you, the air to breathe, "especially in the country", good friends, walks on the beach(if you live by the sea) or any other area where you can relax your mind, giving yourself time to refocus.

Give your mind and body the proper nutrients it needs to not only assist with your emotional well-being but also to have a positive impact on others around you.

Don't let your life be just another one pager but rather a beautiful story to tell.

The essence of life is within your grasp. The question is what you will do to claim your right to your true identity.

PART TWO

Life's Playground

"You're the sum of your choices. You're exactly who, what and where you choose to be in life"

To a kid the word "party, presents", means only one thing, "excitement" and when there is but a sniff of going there, then this excitement graduates to another level of happiness which then becomes their own playground they create in their minds.

This level combined with access to sweets, cool drinks is the perfect environment for any kid to have them live out their wildest dreams of just being kids.

And this playground is filled with fantasies, dreams of being superman, Spiderman etc. which point to the thoughts, ideas of many a small child around the world.

But one thing that they don't yet realize is that this environment is but just part of their preparation for life's true playground, where they also will have access to what this playground has to offer but with one big difference. With this new level they now face, their lives are now depended on the choices they are going to make, with these choices becoming their ultimate pathway to either succeed and enjoy this new environment of life's journey or facing utter failure.

This means the choices springing forth from their new playground as adults will now become the building blocks to shape their futures, whether good or bad.

It sounds very harsh but unfortunately you are the product of the choices you have made.

As I said before with my writing on "the essence of life" I said that your heart is your book of life, with this heart pointing to your emotional well-being which we all know will control your life if this area of your life is in turmoil for whatever reason.

And therefore your emotional well-being will determine your personality. So if we make wrong choices because of our emotional well-being, our book of life not in a good place, that what will come from within is a negative force capable of destroying not just yourself but others around you.

"Being negative from within can become a deadly virus that knows no boundaries."

And this can be because of not making proper use of your playground's library that is available for you to scroll through to pick the proper choices that is there to help you to not just cope with difficult situations that life sometimes can throw at you but to overcome it.

With probably the most important one "your message of someone that is in need of help" is being ignored by yourself.

While watching a program on television about people that faced death after being attacked by predators but survived to share their ordeal, one of these stories captivated me.

This man after being attacked by a hippopotamus faced his most difficult stumbling block in his "life's ladder". He not only lost his left arm but with the scars that this attack clothed him with he saw his whole life, his dreams of building a future with someone to share his life with, having kids, coming to a standstill, since everything turned dark for him at that moment in time.

But one day a doctor he did not know came to him, looked him into the eyes and told him, "You're the product of your choices. You're exactly who, what and where you choose to be in life"

These words encouraged him there and then to start building his life and he did what I call created his "blackboard principle". As you know when in school we all faced a black board where everything was written on and afterwards wiped clean to make room for the next category of information.

So this man dig deep into his playground's library to find the best choice that had to go to the top of his "blackboard" and by making sure he followed through on what he wrote there every time, he was able to build his life.

And not to forget the resources he reached out to with his "message of help"

The most important thing to his success was that his "blackboard" kept talking with him, reminding him to push through, which means through this he created structure, which then propelled him on the path he thought he had lost.

If he had made the wrong choice that day, his life could have meant being caught up in a very dark hole.

Even if he did made the right choice but did not act on his decision because of procrastination, with procrastinating the thief of time he then would have just prolonged the inevitable waiting to happen.

"The different winds don't have a choice from which direction to blow, unlike our choices in life that will determine the course of our lives."

Everyone's playground up until where you are now in life is a result of what you have received not just through your eyes, but ears also, therefore every choice we make comes from what is hidden in your "storage facility"

Therefore the question you have to ask yourself at this very moment.

Are you currently facing the same dark hole this man was facing, feeling the wall of hopelessness, fear, anxiety pressing in, or are you already in this dark place, then the question you must ask yourself, "what decision am I going to make from here to make sure I don't become another victim of this dark and lonely place or while here to get out.

Am I going to apply this blackboard principle to start creating structure to rebuild from within?

Or will I become just another statistic because of not listening to what your "heart, your book of life, your playground" is trying to send out for others to hear, your message of someone in need.

Our whole life is built around the choices we make. Just think at this current moment in time how many choices, thoughts, ideas are busy traveling on the highway of life's playground.

I mean you decide what time to wake up, what to eat, what clothes to wear to work, what time to leave etc. but with every choice you make you make use of the resources available to you.

For example, the moment you are hungry, a message will come from within telling you it is time to eat. This message won't be ignored, so no procrastinating involve here, but the food you eat first of all had to be bought at one of your favorite stores, and the same with your clothes etc.

So this means the sources available in these departments are being properly utilized.

But what about your emotional well-being since it is from here where your happiness will originates from, therefore the way you utilize life's sources will determine how you look at yourself from within.

And this life's sources can have many faces, such as good friends, people you can trust when it comes to advice, quality time for you to refocus, reflect where you are in life etc.

Maybe it is time that you apply the "mirror principle" in your life. See what other people around you see when they look at you. Do they see someone happy or someone pretending to be happy?

So whatever we do in life it all will be to make sure your emotional well-being stays healthy, which means if we make wrong choices because of difficult situations your "heart" will suffer the consequences creating a platform of no happiness from within but rather a nightmare.

Therefore, remember, "You're the sum of your choices; you're exactly who, what and where you choose to be in life."

The Mountain Between Us

"To experience true life, freedom from within, you have to not only remove your chains of yesterday's wrong choices, but utterly destroy in order to activate your access to tomorrow's promises of true happiness".

I can remember in my primary school days the friendship I had with a very special friend who at that time of innocence had big dreams for our futures, with the word "marriage" coming into play.

We were very sure of ourselves of getting married one day that created such a high level of excitement which led to you walking around with this state of mind of what your playground had to offer at that time of what this words "being married" meant.

Not even to mention the fact that the affect this had on you made you felt like a man despite the fact that you were just ten years old.

Now as much as this was just a mere figment of our imagination since we were still very young, it still was just a dream that felt real to us. I mean here were two small kids playing out their dreams of what their playgrounds was providing at that time.

Unfortunately there was one factor that we didn't thought of which was the mountain between us at that time, which inevitably became our mountain of separation between us.

This mountain for us had many faces such as the major one namely "the time factor." I mean we were very young, and with so many things yet to be added to your "storage facility" you eventually grew apart from one another.

And then you had another big problem which is emotional immaturity.

We were too young to play out these dreams of ours, since we lacked the experience of how to not follow our dreams but rather lead it.

Here at this moment at that time we didn't understand the different faces this mountain represented.

I mean how anyone can while in the beginning of their life's journey understand the rules of life properly if they don't have someone to teach and guide them through this process of growing up, so that they can gain knowledge, wisdom and understanding.

And during this you still want to enjoy life as a kid, therefore this barrier separated us from making our dream becoming a reality, our dream of finding our happiness, but it also became our saving grace, all because we were just too young to make such important decisions with your whole life still waiting to be lived.

Today each and everyone have a mountain at this moment in time in their lives. Most people will not admit to it, but unfortunately you cannot live in denial of the truth surrounding your current lives' ladder.

This mountain with its many faces is a reality and we must get rid of it, should we want to experience the full promise of life, which is as I said before is "happiness from within"

Remember the essence of life is not locked up in earthly possessions, or your success in the business world but in your emotional well-being.

The question now will be, but how to get rid of my mountain? The answer is easy. You must become your mountain before you can remove it. In order to understand your problem you need to gain knowledge of it so that you don't just treat the symptoms of what you are struggling with but that what is the major factor behind the symptoms.

This means you must get rid of the root of your problem with this being the reason other people only experience the tip of the iceberg in your life.

"In a world full of problems, be the solution"

The world is filled with problems, but not the problems that most think it is. No I am referring to the different "mountains" out there that is causing so many people to not being able to live up and appreciate what life has to offer.

Too many people have dreams that never become a reality. Many die without completing any of this. And the reason is because of their "mountain" which they did not know how to handle causing them to not knowing how to take ownership of what life has to offer.

Instead of trying to fulfill and complete one dream with the necessary help, too many dreams were flying around all the while you were in war with yourself from within, and just because of not listening to the message of "you in need of help" coming from within, your dreams stayed dreams, with the outcome no evidence on your wall of victory.

What we must understand is that your thinking determines your emotional responses, your behavior, your lifestyle, and the quality of your relationships.

Therefore in order to be successful, to find true happiness, you must become the solution. In order to get rid of the problems in your world, your environment you're living in, which refers to your current lifestyle, you must become the solution to not only identifying, but removing these problem areas successfully.

And this problem is, that what is holding you back, that dead weight you are carrying around, that you are so desperately trying to cope with. That what is hiding in the dark where no one can see it but experience it when the root of your problem has been triggered, with the effects manifesting on the surface?

Remember in part one where I talked about the essence of life that you must become dead on the outside and live on the inside, which means you must increase in life while at the same time will decrease in death.

This means the more you increase in happiness from within, the more that problem that kept you locked away in its clutches of death, that was smothering you so much that hopelessness was starting to become a reality will slowly lose its grip.

But you must remember the most important rule is to follow through with what you have started otherwise this death's clutches will stay there. You must come to this fight with a warrior's attitude otherwise you won't succeed.

And to add another important rule is that there is no room for quick fixes to try and remove this mountain of yours. Quick fixes will not solve your problem whatever it may be. It will only lead to more problems since it is only capable of dealing with the symptoms, and not the root of what is hiding beneath.

No it will take persistence, perseverance to be able to drink from the cup of happiness waiting to be served.

But the question now will be, "But how do I accomplish this? How will I taste victory?

In order to catch a fish I have to do something to first of all lure the fish to where I want it to be. The fish is not going to jump out of the water; no you need bait and a lot of patience for that.

Your problem whatever it is at this moment in time will not jump by itself out from where it is. No you must lure it out. In other words you must become the rod, with the bait the knowledge that you need to remove it from its stronghold.

If you tackle this problem with knowledge of the problem, then you will succeed. But if you go in blind, you will find yourself in a constant battle with yourself, which will lead to unnecessary stress, anxiety and eventually depression which can become a very dark hole.

Therefore when you start to remove this mountain make sure you have someone who you can trust to help you with this challenge. This normally will be someone with experience on these issues. It will be someone who has helped others with similar situations.

Don't try to solve it by yourself, because if you do, you will only lie to yourself about what you are struggling with.

But again it will take hard work, and accountability. Accountability first to yourself since you are the one in search of happiness. I mean you are the one with the problem.

The choice is yours. You can either be accountable and do something about it or irresponsible and ignore it.

And secondly to others around you, and yes so that you can also be well prepared for when you get involved in a relationship, so that your partner can be exposed to the real you.

"Happiness is the cup waiting to be served for those eager to be part of something greater than them"

If you remove your focus from your successes in life, your wealthiness that you worked so hard for, which is nothing wrong with, and take a step back and look at your life where you are at this moment in time, by answering the following question.

Did you during this time of struggling, working long hours, that maybe kept you away from your family gave you happiness from within? Be honest with this answer.

Or are you so addicted to your work or yourself that only you fit into this world. Did this created happiness from within? If it did then why do you shut yourself out from other people?

Happiness from within will bring forth such a positive energy that you will draw people to yourself. Happiness from within will change the way you look at life. You will start to take time to appreciate the small things, which means you will make time for yourself and others important to you.

Just imagine being successful in life while at the same time experience happiness from within. Isn't this what life is about?

And this will be the result of you being successful in removing the mountains in your life that opened the gateway to the essence of life.

So let us summarize what will help you to accomplish happiness from within.

1. Listen to your message of help coming from the inside and act on it. Don't ignore the warning signs.
2. Apply the "Blackboard principle" by writing the best choice your library has to offer at the top and work from there. Make sure this board keeps talking to you.
3. Make sure that you understand what you are dealing with and at the same time have people qualified to help you on this road of finding happiness from within.
4. Most important is to follow through with what you have started. Be persistent and avoid short cuts.

Now I trust with this piece on life's purpose that you will not only understand but realize that true happiness, the riches of life is a reality which is not just meant for a selected few but for everyone who so desire to do something about their mountain standing between them.

So what choices are we going to pick from our library to make this happen.

Happiness from within is
the most precious jewel

The essence of life is not locked
up in earthly possessions but in
your emotional well-being.

Emotional happiness is the gateway to
see and understand the purpose of life.

The way you deal with yesterday will
determine your choices for tomorrow.

The success of your future will be
determined by your obedience to the level
of wisdom, knowledge and understanding
being received from the school of life.

———

To be inspired is the door to discovery
of self, your purpose and abilities.

You're the sum of your choices.
You're exactly who, what and
where you choose to be in life.

———

Your lifestyle can either stab you in the front or the back. You can either see what is coming and do something about it, or know what is coming and ignore it.

Winds don't have a choice from
which direction to blow, unlike our
choices in life that will determine
the course of our lives.

Being negative from within can become a
deadly virus that knows no boundaries.

"In a world full of problems
be the solution"

"Don't follow your dreams, lead it"

"Happiness is the cup waiting to be
served for those eager to be part of
something greater than them"